PRINTED IN THE UNITED STATES OF AMERICA
Signature Book Printing, www.sbpbooks.com

ISBN 978-1-935932-23-9

American Family Publishing
A division of American Family Association
107 Parkgate Drive
Tupelo, MS 38801

afa.net

Unless otherwise noted, Scripture quotations in this book are from the English Standard Version. (All rights reserved. The Holy Bible, English Standard Version® (ESV®) Copyright © 2001 by Crossway, a publishing ministry of Good News Publishers.)

Cover design by Canada Burns

Project oversight by Buddy Smith

A PASTOR'S NOTES
God Calls
the Church to
Stand Boldly
for Life

JOSEPH PARKER

TABLE OF CONTENTS

APPENDIX

ENDORSEMENTS

"*A Pastor's Notes: God Calls the Church to Stand Boldly for Life* is a timely and timeless collection of life affirming articles that will stir pastors to seek and find the courage to lead congregations and communities to embrace the sanctity of life. It is a tool kit must for the discerning servant leaders of today. "

— *Evangelist Alveda King, Director, Civil Rights for The Unborn*
Niece of Dr. Martin Luther King Jr.

"*A Pastor's Notes: God Calls the Church to Stand Boldly for Life* is exceptionally well-written and challenges us as people of faith to stand for life. I particularly like the fact that Rev. Joseph Parker shows his conviction through living out his faith and being persistent in taking a stand with much passion for life. Thank you, Rev. Parker, for a well-researched and well-written book that calls all humanity of the Christian faith to examine the biblical Scriptures and apply truth as God would have us all do with this gift of life."

— *Rev. E. Charles Cotton, Presiding Elder, North District*
South MS Conference, Eighth Episcopal District, African Methodist
Episcopal Church

1

"This is a book of wisdom, wisdom born of pain – the pain of abortion and the study of the Word of God. You can find life, healing, joy, and vision in this book. I encourage everyone to read each life-sized nugget of wisdom."

— *Attorney Allan E. Parker Jr., President, The Justice Foundation*

"I don't know another Christian leader or pastor more committed to ending abortion in our nation. For many years, Joseph Parker has proven himself a steady, prayerful, righteous man of God as he contends for the lives of pre-born babies. If other pastors will listen, Joseph's voice will inspire and challenge them to join him on the spiritual battlefield to save the lives of the children Jesus already knows and loves."

— *Tim Wildmon, President, American Family Association and American Family Radio*

"There are few times that history demands aggressive biblical leadership from a nation's pulpits, and this moment for America is now. I praise God that American Family Association has moved into this moment to provide *A Pastor's Notes: God Calls the Church to Stand Boldly for Life* to help guide clarity and leadership during these trying times of a pro-life movement seeking insight for next steps, and a country frozen by the impact of abortion. *A Pastor's Notes* challenges pastors, spiritual leaders, and the church as a whole to much more fervently get involved with taking a strong stand for protecting life. This book's author, Pastor Joseph Parker, is one of the most profound and consistent voices in the pro-life movement I've met since my epiphany on this issue some 30 years ago. I would implore you to read this small yet powerful book and glean from the wisdom shared."

— *Star Parker, Syndicated Columnist, Author, Founder of UrbanCURE*

"Pastor Joseph Parker challenges faith leaders to share with their congregations the singular reality of human existence – how we're all created in the image and likeness of God. Each blog is a quick read and accessible to everyone. Thank God for Pastor Parker's willingness to unpack the Scriptures and encourage us all to share this important truth."

— *Joe Langfeld, Executive Director, Human Life Alliance*

"This new book by Joseph Parker is important because it shouts a truth that many in the Christian community don't want to hear. Simply put, that truth is that the biggest enemy of unborn life is not Planned Parenthood or the Democratic Party or the ACLU. Instead, it is the indifference and the silence of the church. It is the church's hands that are most stained with blood from over 60 million little boys and girls.

Whatever else you believe about the abortion holocaust, believe this: If even a small percentage of the churches in America were to honestly and fully commit to ending it, the abortion lobby would be powerless to stop them. But for decades, the church has been willing to sit back and be led by popular culture rather than lead it, and the result is the sorry mess our country is in today. It is time to pull our heads out of the sand and recognize that in the cultural civil war that is raging for the future of America, the church is cowering in the shadows.

Dr. Martin Luther King once said about the civil rights movement, "In the end, we will remember not the words of our enemies, but the silence of our friends." Rev. Parker is sounding the same alarm. His book is a warning that, right now, the American church is whistling past its own graveyard. We had better listen."

— *Mark Crutcher, President, Life Dynamics Incorporated*

"This book is an absolute must read for every believer who is in the battle to save the lives of unborn babies.

Joseph has written a book that reveals his character and courage. Many write books, op-eds, and articles that are aimed at people who they know will readily accept and agree with their perspective. This is not the case with Joseph Parker. He has written about a subject that many in his circle would rather he either change his views or keep them to himself. Joseph has done neither. He speaks for the God of the Bible on the sanctity of human life. I pray that all will read this book. It is an indispensable part of every preacher's library!"

— *Bishop Patrick Wooden, pastor of Upper Room COGIC of Raleigh and Bishop of North Carolina Third Jurisdiction of COGIC*

DEDICATION

This book is dedicated to our Lord and Savior, Jesus Christ, who is the Lord of Life. It is our hope He will use it to help save many more of His precious children and end the tragedy of abortion in our culture and our world.

"I call heaven and earth to witness against you today, that I have set before you life and death, blessing and curse. Therefore, choose life, that you and your offspring may live, loving the Lord your God, obeying his voice and holding fast to him, for he is your life and length of days, that you may dwell in the land that the Lord swore to your fathers, to Abraham, to Isaac, and to Jacob, to give them."

— Deuteronomy 30:19-20

"In the beginning was the Word, and the Word was with God, and the Word was God. He was in the beginning with God. All things were made through him, and without him was not any thing made that was made. In him was life, and the life was the light of men."

— John 1:1-4

FOREWORD

Intentional. Persistent. Steeped in the Word of God. Passionate. Hopeful in God that someone will hear, read, and act in the truth and faith of God's Word.

Chapter after chapter in Rev. Joseph Parker's book *A Pastor's Notes: God Calls the Church to Stand Boldly for Life* explores our cultural, religious, and political views to demonstrate through documentation how little value God's world tends to place on life.

Unapologetically, Parker reveals through his articles that his obedience and relationship to God are more important to him than any worldly beliefs/practices that are contrary to the Word of God about life and living life more abundantly. So, against all odds, he persists in telling God's truth. Through his articles and his daily works of pastoring and being involved in a variety of community and national family life projects, he cuts directly to the core of the issue of life in his stand on abortion, which he declares is murder. Unflinchingly, he proclaims truth as he details ways to inform God's people on the matter of saving God's precious gift of life.

Parker turns the tables on issues held so firmly by the majority culture as shown in courts of the land, in religious denominations, and in government affairs. He posits situations for readers to ponder and weigh as they tend to remain silent on truth matters that are unpopular among the majority. He acknowledges that the truth hurts, but he assures the reader based on biblical principles that God heals hurt and saves us by His grace.

In our quest for freedom, Parker stands firmly on Scripture that *God's truth makes us free*. The slogan *Choose Life* is not just a good sounding imperative statement to chant loudly in public or to display on beautifully designed signs or placards. Our choosing life is *a mandate from God*. This gift of life is the greatest gift from God ... a precious life with which we are to magnify God and accomplish His purpose here on earth.

My hope is that Parker's insights will reach across the globe to penetrate the hearts and minds of all of God's people. The messages cut like a two-edged sword, causing me to ponder more deeply my values about life and my relationship to God. Hebrews 4:12 (NIV) assures, "For the word of God is alive and active. Sharper than any double-edged sword, it penetrates even to dividing soul and spirit, joints and marrow; it judges the thoughts and attitudes of the heart."

My prayer is that one day, Rev. Joseph Parker, as well as all hearts that his words might pierce, will see the work of God through his labors of love for life.

Shirley Hopkins Davis, Ph.D.
8th Connectional Women's Missionary Society President
African Methodist Episcopal Church

8

INTRODUCTION

One of the key elements of authentic Christianity is conviction. By that I mean an unshakable and immutable certainty about who Jesus Christ is and what He expects of His followers. Before Paul went into detail about each facet of the spiritual armor God expects all Christians to be adorned with, he said, "[T]ake up the whole armor of God, that you may be able to withstand in the evil day, and having done all, to stand firm" (Ephesians 6:13, ESV).

Today's church has conceded too much territory to Satan and the culture he presses and drives. In the name of ecumenism and pluralism, many have made theological, doctrinal, and rational concessions to the world in order to be accepted. Fewer and fewer in number are those who are willing "to stand firm" about God's revelation of Himself and His will as revealed in the Bible.

Pastor Joseph Parker is one of those few.

In the pages that follow, you will see both his righteous loathing of abortion as well as his ardent fervor for the sanctity of life. Joseph Parker is standing for the unborn unflinchingly. As editor of The Stand, it has been a joy and a privilege to post his blogs for the world to read.

These are individual blogs that have been posted on The

Stand over the course of six years. Each blog stands on its own merit, but collectively they reveal a flowing stream of adamant conviction about the issue of life.

The goal of this collection of Parker's blogs is to rouse a similar passion for the sanctity of life as it relates to the unborn. But it is also to provide those who are leaders in today's churches with a valuable resource for how and why to enter the fray of this battle and what to do once engaged "against the cosmic powers over this present darkness" (Ephesians 6:12).

This isn't just about promoting or defending a religious belief or doctrine. This is about real flesh and blood human beings who are being wiped out right under our noses and in front of our faces. More than 60 million lives have been taken in America alone since the infamous *Roe v. Wade* decision in 1973.

Read this compilation of blogs. Become knowledgeable and informed. But most of all, become convicted and find a way to make a difference!

Ray Rooney, D.Min.
AFA Digital Media Editor
afa.net/thestand

Church and the Issue of Life

What should we do about the life issue? Should we preach or teach about it, or should we avoid it so that we don't hurt feelings and open old wounds? If we preach and address it, would people be offended? Should we avoid controversial issues such as the life issue and abortion? Shouldn't we preach and teach *only* about culturally acceptable topics that will encourage people? These are questions and issues that the church as a whole and the local church, in particular, should address.

We must preach and teach the truth in love (Ephesians 4:15). We are not called to condemn but to proclaim the truth to a world deceived by the darkness of lies. If we fail to preach and teach truth, people will be lost and ultimately die in their sins. So often important life decisions are based on what is deemed culturally and socially acceptable. But culture and society are usually deceived because they do not love or embrace the truth.

While preaching and teaching are powerful tools to wield, we must do more. We must also aggressively provide ministry to pregnant women in their time of need. What can be done? We can vigorously come alongside the ministries of local pregnancy centers.

Many believers in the church are not aware of the powerful work pregnancy centers do in the local community. They provide a safe, loving, and warm environment for women in crisis pregnancies. They love these women by providing wise and positive counseling concerning ways to get the help they need to either keep their baby or lovingly place their baby up for adoption. They usually provide their services at no charge and often provide free baby items for expecting mothers.

Many also are not aware that much evangelism, discipleship, and pastoral care are given to women and their families through the ministry of pregnancy clinics. A director of one pregnancy center in the Mississippi Delta shared with me that around 500 persons had accepted Christ over the years. So the question becomes, how can the local church get involved?

For starters we can begin to see the local pregnancy center as an extension of the church. A church fellowship can decide to do some or all of the following things to support, encourage, and help the work of local pregnancy centers:

1. Pray daily and faithfully for the ministry of your local pregnancy center. Much spiritual warfare happens at these centers.

2. Give generously to the work of your local pregnancy center, either a single generous gift or place them in your church's annual budget.

3. Regularly recruit and send volunteers from your church to help at your local pregnancy center.

4. Donate baby items to your local pregnancy center: diapers, baby clothes, baby accessories, etc.

5. Regularly inquire about other ways your church fellowship can help.

Local churches can also prayerfully consider beginning or sponsoring a post-abortion healing Bible study. In view of the fact that one in every three or four women has had an abortion in our culture, the number of people who are hurting from this tragedy is *staggering*! The sheer number of abortions is such that it necessarily must touch every single congregation in the country! Not to seek to provide the ministry of forgiveness and healing for these men and women would be negligent on our part. Forgiveness and healing are born in the Word of God ... so start a Bible study!

Finally, have creative events where the issue of life is addressed in a biblical, practical, and loving way. Host events that educate believers about this issue from a scriptural perspective. Use the Sanctity of Human Life Sunday in January to do much spiritual education about this topic. Also, you could host a Festival for Life.*

These are only a few suggestions. There are many more things churches can do to intentionally and faithfully address the life issue. Pray for the Lord to guide you and your church family to do what He would have you do to stand faithfully for life this year and beyond.

*A Festival for Life is a multimedia, family-friendly event that uses movie clips, music videos, and movie trailers to help share a biblical message. Through this presentation we share about the need for the

13

church to biblically and aggressively support the work of pregnancy clinics and stand for life. If you are interested in bringing this event to your church or community, you may call AFA at 662.844.5036 x381.

Originally posted 1/12/2016

Doing God's Word to Avoid
Self-Deception

We live in a world where lip service to God and the Word of God is very common, yet people's actions tell the story of what they truly believe and stand for.

The Word of God is truth. As we read and study the Word, we are confronted with the truth. Yet it is critical we understand that truth is not meant to simply be read and acknowledged. Truth is always meant to be applied. And when truth is applied, it sets us free.

God's Word tells us, *"But be doers of the Word, and not hearers only, deceiving yourselves"* (James 1:22).

There are many people who say they love the Lord and say that the Word of God is their guide. Yet clearly too many of them are not genuinely guided by the wisdom and counsel of the Word of God. People who do this may believe it's acceptable in their minds to read the Word of God even as they make excuses as to why they can ignore what that Word is saying. When they do this, they are deceiving themselves.

If a married man attends church regularly, reads the Bible regularly, and says he loves the Lord, yet he consistently commits adultery, he is deceiving himself. Though he may be reading the Word of God, he is not a doer of the Word in his life.

What if that man says, "It's no big deal, as long as I don't get

15

caught?" If that's what he believes, does that mean that what he is doing is not a sin? Does that mean his actions are now no longer wrong? No, it means that he is committing adultery, and he is deceiving himself.

If a woman or man is a faithful student of the Word of God, reading every day – yet he or she is a habitual shoplifter – what does this say about this man or woman? He or she is consistently stealing, yet goes to church. That person is a thief. He or she is clearly disobeying the command *"You shall not steal"* (Exodus 20:15).

A person may say, "This company is big, and they will never miss the few things I take. Besides, I'm not stealing – I'm just permanently borrowing." Because this person has reasoned in his or her heart that what they are doing is not wrong and is not a sin, does that mean their thinking is true? No, this person is also breaking the commandment *"You shall not steal"* (Exodus 20:15).

If a pregnant woman says, "I am not killing anybody, I'm just exercising my reproductive rights by getting rid of this baby," does that mean that her abortion is not a sin? The Word of God clearly says, *"You shall not murder"* (Exodus 20:13). If she does have her child aborted, it is an act of murder. It is clearly disobeying the Word of God.

The Word of God mercifully lets us know: *"If we confess our sins, He is faithful and just to forgive us our sins and to cleanse us from all unrighteousness"* (1 John 1:9).

God is very willing to forgive someone of any of these wrongs if a person confesses and repents of them.

So, when people say they respect the Word of God, reverence the Word and read it, yet do not attempt to obey it, they have deceived themselves. The Word of God is truth.

Yet truth is always meant to be applied. The Bible was never meant to be a souvenir. It's a guidebook for all of life. Let us strive to always be hearers and doers of the Word of God.

Originally posted 3/2/2020

Babies and Politics: Pharaoh, Herod, and Presidential Candidates

Leaders, or aspiring leaders, who feel that babies, when unwanted, can and should be disposed of – legally – are examples we've seen before in the Bible.

Pharaoh, the mighty king of ancient Egypt, and Herod the King who reigned as the ruler of Judea are just two. Exodus 1:15-18 is Pharaoh's story in the Old Testament:

> *Then the king of Egypt said to the Hebrew midwives, one of whom was named Shiphrah and the other Puah, "When you serve as midwife to the Hebrew women and see them on the birthstool, if it is a son, you shall kill him, but if it is a daughter, she shall live." But the midwives feared God and did not do as the king of Egypt commanded them, but let the male children live.*
>
> *So the king of Egypt called the midwives and said to them, "Why have you done this, and let the male children live?"*

Herod took a similar action in Matthew 2:16:

> *Then Herod, when he saw that he had been tricked by the wise men, became furious, and he sent and killed all the male children in Bethlehem and in all that region who*

were two years old or under, according to the time that he
had ascertained from the wise men.

Many may react and say, "How dare you compare any of our presidential candidates to these ancient tyrants – these barbarians!" Yet the comparison is not only appropriate, it's one that we, in the church in particular and in our culture as a whole, need to take a long and hard look at.

When we consider the history of what these wicked leaders did for their own selfish, cruel, and heartless reasons, it is easy to criticize them. However, consider this: If we notice many of the candidates for the office of president of the United States of America have the same perspective towards unwanted children in the womb and even some who are just delivered, then we have a great reason to pause.

Many of these candidates have very large followings. They have many people who support them just as they are – baby killer perspective and all. This reality is one of the greatest tragedies of presidential campaigns.

Tragically, these candidates reflect the hearts and thinking of those who follow them. We are living in a world where we can easily look at history and look at many other leaders as well as the two mentioned, and be angry, critical, and horrified at the masses of people that they murdered.

However, if you are supporting a leader who thinks, acts, and supports such perspectives, where does that place you as a human being? What does that say about your own character? What does that say about who you are siding with in the context of all of history?

Many will say, "Well, abortion is just one single issue – there are other issues just as important if not more important than this one issue! One issue is not greater than the others."

Like the slavery issue in the elections of the mid-1800s, the abortion issue towers above all others.

If the lives of millions of babies are snuffed out, what does it matter that the economy is good? If millions of the most innocent U.S. citizens can be legally murdered, foreign policy is insignificant for them. For the precious babies whose lives were cut short, the creation of new jobs won't matter. They will not be here to live, love, and serve God. They will not be here to fill the jobs, pay into the economy, or pay taxes.

If you lived in the mid-1800s, and the candidate you favored had excellent ideas and perspectives on almost all the issues important to you, was brilliant, articulate, and passionate about his message but supported slavery, would you decide that slavery was just one "small" issue that could be overlooked? Would you push this reality to the side? Or would you decide that this one issue is big enough to overshadow all the rest of the virtues of this individual?

My hope is that you would be wise enough to understand that some issues clearly are much bigger in importance than others. Some issues are greater in importance, impact, and in the magnitude of the consequences that will be produced.

The Word of God tells us in one of the Ten Commandments, *"You shall not murder"* (Exodus 20:13). Also, in Deuteronomy 30:19, God tells us to *"choose life that you and your offspring may live."* Where do you stand?

Originally posted 2/17/2020

20

Abortion: First Degree Murder

In Exodus chapter 20, the Lord gave us the Ten Commandments. These are 10 foundational truths that will bless us, our families, our societies, and our world if we will adhere to them and choose to live by the wisdom found in them. They were given for our good to make life better for us.

These commandments honor God and bless the people who live according to them. To violate them is to dishonor God and bring trouble, difficulty, and death upon the disobedient. It is in our best interest to hear, obey, and live by each of the Ten Commandments. Each one blesses our lives in a unique way.

The sixth commandment says, *"You shall not murder."* This commandment, perhaps more than any other commandment, has extreme consequences when it is violated. One key reason is, when it is violated, a human being is taken out of this world. An individual made in the image of God is no longer in this world as a result of the actions of one or more other human beings.

Abortion is a form of murder – plain and simple. More specifically, abortion is first-degree murder. It is not accidental, but typically well-planned. Tragically, there are much deception, misleading, and lies surrounding abortion. Sadly, many who say they are believers are taking the word "murder" and seeking to substitute it with words like "abortion," "reproductive rights," and "euthanasia." It seems that they want to believe that murder is acceptable if we rename it. Yet whatever name you give the act of taking innocent life, it is still clearly wrong according to the Word of God. Abortion is murder. It's clearly against the Word and will of God.

Sadly, because this specific kind of murder has been repackaged, rebranded, and sold to our culture with a brand new face and cover, many have bought into it. So much so that now it's been stated that one out of every three or four women has had an abortion. We have become a nation of murderers.

"That's a very harsh way to put it," one might say. Well, sometimes the hard truth hurts. Sometimes it's a very hard pill to swallow. Yet sometimes being faced with the hard truth head-on helps us to wake up and see where we are and what we are.

Now the God we serve is merciful and full of loving-kindness and forgiveness. He clearly tells us in His Word, *"If we confess our sins, He is faithful and just to forgive us our sins and cleanse us from all unrighteousness"* (1 John 1:9).

We serve a wonderful heavenly Father who majors in forgiveness. Our job is to confess when we have done wrong, repent, and ask for Him to forgive us. He will certainly do it. He always keeps His Word.

So, is abortion really first-degree murder? Yes, it is. And there are already laws on the books against that. God's Word never changes. We did. We allowed ourselves to be deceived and lulled to sleep.

So what should we do? We need to be wise enough, bold enough, and committed enough to say that we have been wrong about the whole matter of abortion. It always has been and always will be wrong to commit first-degree murder. God's Word will never change.

"I call heaven and earth to witness against you today, that I have set before you life and death, blessing and curse. Therefore, choose life, that you and your offspring may live" (Deuteronomy 30:19).

Originally posted 3/29/2019

The Dangerous Idol of Abortion

Why is legalized abortion so important to so many people? Sadly, many people have made abortion an idol. They "worship" the golden calf of abortion and are willing to fight tooth and nail to keep it in place. For a lot of people, abortion is a big money-making business. For others, it's an easy way out of a difficult circumstance. Many people want to keep it in place so they can keep their "financial benefits" while others depend on it as a "convenient" tool to use whenever and however they "need" it. Consequently, their perspective is, "Don't you dare even think about overturning *Roe v. Wade!*"

I believe that we, the church, should be diligent and passionate about faithfully doing at least five things:

1. Stand firmly on the truths of God's Word and trust the Lord.

2. Pray without ceasing in spiritual combat.

3. Faithfully and passionately support and stand with the work of pregnancy clinics.

4. Faithfully speak out against abortion and have events that speak passionately about the life issue.

5. Listen to the Holy Spirit as to what else we need to do to boldly stand for life.

What should the church's stand be on the life issue? How should we decide what side to stand on? The answer is very simple. What does the Word of God say? In Exodus 20:13, we read: "*You shall not murder.*" This is very clear and to the point. Murder is the taking of innocent life.

How sad it is that people have too often been misled when deceivers will substitute the word murder with more "acceptable" terms. Words such as "abortion," "reproductive rights," and "euthanasia" may not sound quite as harsh as murder. Yet the result is the same. Innocent life is deliberately taken.

We are wise to hear the clear, direct, and profound counsel of God's Word that helps us know very plainly what His will is in this matter. The Lord tells us in His Word:

> "*I call heaven and earth to witness against you today, that I have set before you life and death, blessing and curse. Therefore choose life, that you and your offspring may live*" (Deuteronomy 30:19).

God, our heavenly Father knows us better than we know ourselves. He is certainly full of mercy, grace, and lovingkindness. He is a restoring Shepherd.

God's Word tells us, *"If we confess our sins, He is faithful and just to forgive us our sins and to cleanse us from all unrighteousness"* (1 John 1:9).

When we sin, if we acknowledge and confess it, and turn from it in genuine repentance, and ask Him to forgive us, He will. He will forgive the sin of abortion and other sins as well.

May we, the church of Jesus Christ, not rest until the idol of abortion is torn down and destroyed.

Originally posted 1/27/2020

The Ten Commandments and the Supreme Court

The law of the LORD is perfect, reviving the soul; the testimony of the LORD is sure, making wise the simple; the precepts of the LORD are right, rejoicing the heart; the commandment of the LORD is pure, enlightening the eyes; the fear of the LORD is clean, enduring forever; the rules of the LORD are true, and righteous altogether. More to be desired are they than gold, even much fine gold; sweeter also than honey and drippings of the honeycomb. Moreover, by them is your servant warned; in keeping them there is great reward (Psalm 19:7-11).

Who decides what is right and what is wrong? Leaders in government? The Supreme Court? "Spiritual" leaders? Parents? The educational system? Culture? Celebrities? Or is it the news and the media?

None of the above. God decides what is right and what is wrong. In His Word, He teaches us His heart and perspective. God's Word is what is right. And it is eternal (which means that it never changes).

The Ten Commandments are from the heart and mind of God. They teach us what is right and wrong. They don't change. People's decisions, thinking, and perspectives all change – but the Word of God doesn't. The Word of God is Jesus, and Jesus is the same yesterday, today, and forever (Hebrews 13:8). He shows us the way to go: "Your word is a lamp to my feet and a light to my path" (Psalm 119:105).

The Ten Commandments contain eternal wisdom, insight, and understanding concerning God and our relationship to Him. They also contain insight about life and our relationship with other people. They contain insight about ownership and property and how to honor God in how we see and care for people and their property.

The Supreme Court in our nation is the highest court in the United States. It is held in high esteem, and the members of the Supreme Court serve in a very honorable and esteemed position in our judicial branch of government.

However, it is important that we always remember that the Supreme Court is not the Supreme Court. God is. God is the Supreme Court, He is the Supreme Justice.

His Word is final and does not change.

Men and women, no matter how highly esteemed and honorable their positions might be, are fallible and make mistakes. The history of the Supreme Court is not flawless. Terrible decisions have been made.

One was the *Dred Scott* decision (*Dred Scott v. Sanford*) in which the court decided that black people were not considered American citizens with standing in court and that Congress could not ban slavery.

That Supreme Court decision was superseded by two amendments to the U.S. Constitution. They are the 13th Amendment, which abolished slavery, and the 14th Amendment, which guaranteed citizenship for all persons born or naturalized in the U.S.

The Supreme Court's *Dred Scott* decision is denounced by scholars. Three modern scholars – Bernard Schwartz, Junius P. Rodriguez, and David T. Konig – all believe that the *Dred Scott* decision was the Supreme Court's worst decision ever.

The Supreme Court also made a grave error in the case of *Plessy v. Ferguson* when it chose to uphold the separate but equal doctrine. Through their decision, the court basically indicated that racial segregation was supported by the U.S. Constitution. A later Supreme Court decision (*Brown v. Board of Education*) effectively overturned *Plessy*.

In *Roe v. Wade*, the Supreme Court decided that abortion is a constitutional right. Sadly, it is still the law of the land with more than 60 million children as casualties despite the fact that the Word of God clearly states, "*You shall not murder.*"

Trends and culture cannot overturn the will of God. And no human court – no matter how "supreme" it claims to be – can overrule God. When the leaders in government are wise enough to recognize that the Supreme Judge of the universe is wiser than they are, many good things can and will happen in our nation. May we as a nation be wise enough to pray for and put in office leaders who know and follow the only King of Kings and Lord of Lords.

Originally posted 10/16/2019

The Insane Culture Against Life

So many people in the world we live in appear to have gone crazy.

We have seen the tragedies of mass shootings in churches, stores, schools, workplaces, and night clubs. Each time we are shocked when they appear in the news.

What are the causes behind these tragedies? Why do we have so many people who are choosing to murder others? Where does this kind of thinking come from? What is in the hearts of those who choose to take the lives of others including some they don't even know?

A very important part of the answer can be found as we ask ourselves this question: What values and ideas about life are we teaching children and our people as a whole? What message does our culture consistently teach us about life and the value of life?

Our perspectives, thinking, and views should come from the Word of God.

God's Word clearly tells us, *"You shall not murder"* (Exodus 20:13). Each of the Ten Commandments shares wisdom to help us in every area of our lives. God's Word also says:

I call heaven and earth to witness against you today, that I have set before you life and death, blessing and curse. Therefore, choose life, that you and your offspring may live (Deuteronomy 30:19).

God is the giver of life. No one should ever think he or she can deliberately murder another human being at will. We cannot create life from clay. Why should we think that it's ok to take it?

One kind of murder is mourned and viewed as a tragedy. Another kind, abortion, is promoted, encouraged, and celebrated by many. Why?

Is there any connection between mass shootings and abortion? Actually, there is – very much so. The spirit of death and darkness is behind both of them. Satan relishes and promotes death and murder on every front where he can.

Culture teaches lessons that devalue life, so it should be no surprise those who truly embrace those lessons, whether from video games, movies, or the media, actually live them out. Look at the lessons we are hearing, the dark values being taught.

When my wife was ministering to a group of young children she asked them what they were thankful for. Some responded with the expected things:

"I'm thankful for my family."

"I'm thankful for my mom."

"I'm thankful for my home."

However, two little boys, both younger than seven years of age, each said: "I'm thankful my mama didn't abort me." Sadly, they both knew what abortion is and were grateful they were not victims. They were probably aware that perhaps a brother or sister or cousin or friend was not here because of abortion.

So, a couple of questions need to be asked: What kind of world have we made for our children? What messages are they receiving from adults? One message is that adults keep some children, and adults kill some children.

Mother Teresa, in her speech at the 1994 Prayer Breakfast in Washington, DC. said the following:

> But I feel that the greatest destroyer of peace today is abortion, because it is a war against the child, a direct killing of the innocent child, murder by the mother herself. And if we accept that a mother can kill even her own child, how can we tell other people not to kill one another?

Those boys' gratefulness might be considered the voice of millions never given a chance. We are told in Proverbs 31:8-9, *"Open your mouth, judge righteously, defend the rights of the poor and needy."*

We, the church of Jesus Christ, need to pray very deliberately and passionately for the healing of our land. We should also pray that people will come to know Christ and be saved. Once people are saved they can begin to live out the truths God's Word teaches about loving people and valuing life (Mark 12:29-31).

We also need to pray for the ending of legalized abortion. We must boldly speak up and speak out for those precious babies who cannot speak for themselves. We need to repent for the bloodshed in our nation and cry out to God to pour out His healing on our land. This needs to become a high priority for the church today.

Why?

Because the holocaust of abortion has continued to happen on our watch. We must have the will and the Holy Spirit empowered passion to do our part. With God's help, we can end this.

Also, the church needs to make it a high priority to teach all of our children and adults the wisdom of God's Word about loving people. We need to teach the Ten Commandments. If the seed of the Word of God is planted in our hearts, we will see the fruit. We would see more people who respect life standing against every kind of murder.

As we do this, we will see the tragedy of mass shootings diminish. Each form of respecting innocent life encourages the other and so abortion and mass shootings will fade away.

Let's all pray. And let's all learn and teach the wisdom of God's Word that teaches us to love our neighbor as we love ourselves (Mark 12:31). Let us also faithfully live and teach the wisdom of the Ten Commandments (Exodus 20:1-17). This is a task every single one of us can carry out.

Encourage and invite all believers to go to themoraloutcry. com and sign the petition. Let us, by God's mercy, wisdom, grace, and power, end legalized abortion. Let's help stop the murders, abortions, and mass shootings from sea to shining sea.

Originally posted 8/7/2019

Praying for the President

First of all, then, I urge that supplications, prayers, intercessions, and thanksgivings be made for all people, for kings and all who are in high positions, that we may lead a peaceful and quiet life, godly and dignified in every way. This is good, and it is pleasing in the sight of God our Savior, who desires all people to be saved and to come to the knowledge of the truth (1 Timothy 2:1-4).

So Joshua did as Moses told him, and fought with Amalek, while Moses, Aaron, and Hur went up to the top of the hill. Whenever Moses held up his hand, Israel prevailed, and whenever he lowered his hand, Amalek prevailed. But Moses' hands grew weary, so they took a stone and put it under him, and he sat on it, while Aaron and Hur held up his hands, one on one side, and the other on the other side. So his hands were steady until the going down of the sun. And Joshua overwhelmed Amalek and his people with the sword (Exodus 17:10-13).

Extremely intense and relentless spiritual warfare. That's how we really need to see the work of praying and interceding for the president of our nation. We need to pray for him and all other leaders as well. We need to see the critical importance of the church in prayer doing kingdom work for God.

Why is this so important? One reason is given in 1 Timothy 2:2 as we are clearly and directly told to pray for *"for kings and all who are in high positions."* Donald Trump is the president of the United States. We need to pray faithfully for him every day in obedience to the Word of God. If so many believers spent just a portion of the time praying for him that they spend complaining about and criticizing the president, there would be a lot more prayers being lifted up, and much more good would be accomplished.

The opposition to this president is very intense and much of it doesn't even make a lot of sense – at least not in the natural. The media, the opposing political party, the political party that he is in – it appears that opposition is coming against him from almost every side. It seems that there are those who don't like him, no matter what he does.

But when you look at it for what it is, it makes a lot of sense. From a spiritual perspective and from a spiritual warfare perspective, it makes plenty of sense.

President Trump is far from perfect, like all the rest of us. That's not even a question here. Yet he has made it a point to commit to carrying out certain mandates – a number of which line up with the counsel from the Word of God.

He has taken a strong stand against abortion – in word and in action – which is consistent with the command not to murder (Exodus 20:13). He also seems to make decisions that are genuinely in the best interest of our nation as a whole (1 Kings 3:9). He has officially recognized Jerusalem as Israel's capital, showing adherence to the words *"Pray for the peace of Jerusalem: they shall prosper that love thee*" (Psalm 122:6).

These are the kinds of accomplishments that make him very unpopular with the devil and the kingdom of darkness. So the onslaught of opposition continues.

Yet the work of the church is clear. We are called to pray for our president and other leaders in authority. We need to be consistent, fervent, and persevering in prayer. The success of the president is directly connected to how faithfully the church is praying for him (Exodus 17:8-13).

Let's be about our Father's business. Let's keep the president lifted up in intense prayer every day.

Originally posted 5/30/2019

Coronavirus: Judgment because of Abortion?

A CNN report (dated 4/9/2020) was titled "Abortion access thrown into jeopardy by coronavirus pandemic." The report said, "Abortion provider Marie Stopes International, which operates across 37 countries, has warned of far-reaching impacts worldwide if women's reproductive rights are not protected as governments limit citizens' activities."

The question needs to be asked here: What would be the far-reaching impact of women not being able to get abortions and abortion services being curtailed? Obviously, babies would be born alive and well.

The report was clearly interested in protecting women's reproductive rights. Well, what about the need to protect the rights of the children from being murdered in their mother's womb?

The report further stated, "Our initial projections warn that unless governments act now, up to 9.5 million vulnerable women and girls risk losing access to our contraception and safe abortion services in 2020 due to the COVID-19 pandemic. The consequences would be devastating."

Some additional questions that should be asked include: In view of the fact that this report speaks of safe abortion services, what is safe about a procedure that, when carried out, always kills a human being? What is so "devastating" about giving children the opportunity to be born and live productive lives?

The tragedies, the ironic truths, the lies, the deception of news media in cooperation with the wicked abortion industry, and its agenda are all sad realities.

Some governmental leaders have taken steps to order many non-essential businesses and activities to close for a time during the coronavirus pandemic and understandably so. Yet some of those same leaders have allowed abortion clinics to continue to operate, saying the services that they provide are "essential."

Think about that. Leaders have taken great steps to close down much of our society in order to preserve human lives. Yet what does abortion do? It *takes* human lives.

How can anyone think that killing children in the womb is "essential?"

A recent article in the Washington Examiner states that the coronavirus exposes Planned Parenthood's biggest lie. A notice from a Pennsylvania branch of Planned Parenthood stated, "To ensure the health and safety of our patients, staff, and community, Planned Parenthood Keystone has temporarily closed all of its health centers for family planning visits effective March 23, 2020."

The notice went on to say, "At this time, Planned Parenthood Keystone is serving patients in Allentown, Wilkes-Barre, Warminster, Reading, York, and Harrisburg for abortion services only."

If Planned Parenthood is committed to women's health as it tries to claim that it is, why close the health care centers at this time and keep the abortion clinics open?

Another Planned Parenthood clinic in Pennsylvania said,

"Effective March 25, 2020, we have temporarily closed our Health Centers to ensure the health and safety of our patients, staff, and community."

Yet, above that same notice, a sign said, "COVID-19 UPDATE: Our Abortion Centers are open!"

It is so tragic that people who are pro-abortion are both aggressive and dedicated to their sad cause. They believe that helping women avoid the "perceived" inconvenience of a nine-month pregnancy is much more important than the life of a precious baby girl or boy.

Pregnancy should never be seen as an "inconvenience." It is a divine gift from God our heavenly Father.

Many other women long to receive and experience the gift of pregnancy. Yet, for whatever reason, they may never receive it. Without question, the experience of bearing and carrying children in the womb is a great and precious gift. What a tragedy abortion is in view of the fact that it devastates pregnancy. And sadly, many women who choose to abort may never be able to have children again.

Attorney and minister Allan Parker, the president of the Justice Foundation, recently stated, "The coronavirus is a judgment of God for the shedding of innocent blood."

Also, recently I heard a sermon on a radio broadcast, in which a Methodist pastor stated that the Lord had told her that the coronavirus has come upon us because of abortion. Well, the Word of God clearly tells us that we reap what we sow:

> *Do not be deceived: God is not mocked, for whatever one sows, that will he also reap. For the one who sows to his own flesh will from the flesh reap corruption, but the one*

who sows to the Spirit will from the Spirit reap eternal life (Galatians: 6:7).

Abortion is the deliberate taking of innocent human life. Tragically, more than 60 million babies have died in the U.S. since 1973. We as a nation have sown many seeds of death by promoting and carrying out abortions. It appears that the coronavirus may very well be our nation reaping the harvest from the seeds of abortion down through the years.

Individuals, families, communities, states, and nations are all taking steps to be careful and wise to preserve health and life. Many of us are wearing masks, washing our hands, being careful to disinfect things, etc. Why? Because we want to preserve life and health. Babies in the womb cannot take steps on their own behalf to preserve their lives. They have neither the understanding nor ability in their situation to do so. They are totally dependent upon their mothers to take steps to protect them. Abortion is a conscious and intentional decision to kill them.

Our sovereign heavenly Father sees and knows what's going on. Look at Jeremiah 19:4-5:

> [T]hey have forsaken Me and have made this an alien place and have burned sacrifices in it to other gods, that neither they nor their forefathers nor the kings of Judah had ever known, and ... they have filled this place with the blood of the innocent and have built the high places of Baal to burn their sons in the fire as burnt offerings to Baal, a thing which I never commanded or spoke of, nor did it ever enter My mind.

40

Look also at Ezekiel 16:20-21:

Moreover, you took your sons and daughters whom you had borne to me and sacrificed them to idols to be devoured. Were your harlotries so small a matter? You slaughtered my children and offered them up to idols by causing them to pass through the fire.

Now, we need to always be mindful of this great truth. We serve a merciful and forgiving heavenly Father. In 1 John 1:9, we are told, *"If we confess our sins, He is faithful and just to forgive us our sins and to cleanse us from all unrighteousness."*

Without question, if we confess and repent of our sin, including the sin of abortion, and ask for his forgiveness, He will forgive us and cleanse us from all unrighteousness. God is full of mercy and lovingkindness. If we simply come to Him and bring this matter, He will receive us, forgive us, and heal us.

Yet how important it is that we come to recognize that killing our children should never be our choice. We must repent of this sin and stop aborting God's precious children.

Great is the need for us as individual believers and as the church to repent of our apathy or negligence of adequately and faithfully taking a bold stand for life against abortion. Lord, forgive us and help us as your people now to stand up boldly and speak up and speak out for life.

Abortion activists are unrelenting in furthering their agenda. We, the church, should be even more aggressive than the kingdom of darkness. Let us, through our prayers, our words, our witness, our actions, and our bold stance, seek to end the tragedy of legalized abortion today.

Originally posted 4/28/20

Murder is Not a Human Right

Pro-abortion legislators introduced a very tragic bill in the U.S. House of Representatives in December 2018. It is a bill that would force the government to declare the killing of unborn babies a "human right."

The pro-abortion bill, (Reproductive Rights are Human Rights Act of 2018), would require the U.S. State Department to include abortion on demand in its annual human rights report. Think about that for a moment – abortion – a human right? Abortion is deliberately taking the life of a baby in his or her mother's womb. A baby is an innocent life. That makes abortion a form of murder.

The Word of God says in Exodus 20:13, *"You shall not murder."* This is the sixth of the Ten Commandments. It is a clear command and directive from the heart of God our heavenly Father. Murder is the taking of innocent life.

Throughout history, mankind has all too often substituted its own will for God's whenever God's will got in the way of mankind's wants and desires. We are prone to bend and twist the perfect and eternal Word in order to justify our perverse desires.

When murder becomes a "human right," then no "right" is out of bounds or off limits. Anything goes! The list of "rights" that people could come up with is potentially endless.

Throughout history, we have seen leaders change "murder" into "cleansings." Men like Hitler, Stalin, Pol Pot, etc. turned murder into a "solution." This is what happens when we turn away from the eternal truth of "Thus saith the Lord." God's Word is good for all people, cultures, communities, and nations. Violating His Word leads to loss, trouble, heartache, and death. Calling disobedience to God a "human right" is utterly and profoundly disastrous.

One final important truth to be considered is this. One of the great needs in our culture is for bold believers to stand courageously and without apology speaking and standing on the Word of God. Technology, culture, and societal mores change often and rapidly. But truth as revealed in Scripture never changes. The sixth commandment stands no matter what culture says or which "right" people demand.

Originally posted 1/15/2019

Life and the Litmus Test

The term "litmus test" is used very often in our political culture. One definition of a litmus test is a test that uses a single indicator to prompt a decision. It's a tool that many politicians and people use to select who or what they will support. Normally, a litmus test involves a matter about which people will have very serious and strong convictions.

So, should people who consider themselves to be believers in Jesus Christ have a litmus test about supporting life and taking a stand against abortion? Should they use such a test to decide whether or not to support and vote for political candidates? The answer is a profound "yes."

Though litmus tests are usually frowned upon because they tend to be oriented around a single factor, there are reasons for their use that are simple and profound. Especially when considering the issue of life in the context of the abortion debate.

For instance, one of the Ten Commandments clearly says, *"You shall not murder"* (Exodus 20:13). This commandment is very clear and straightforward. Bear in mind that the Word of God does not change. Even if you choose to use words or terms like "abortion," "a woman's right to choose," "reproductive rights," "euthanasia," etc., it is still murder.

Changing the name or terms of how you describe what is taking place does not make it anything but an act of disobedience to the will of God. No matter what you call it, it is still murder.

If a leader is not willing to stand up to protect and respect the life and civil rights of the most *innocent and helpless* of his or her own citizens, what does it matter what he or she believes about the economy, job creation, foreign policy, or anything else? If a given person is dead, none of these issues matter at all.

If a candidate believes that an entire segment of the population can be legally murdered, what does that say about her or his character? Doesn't it actually say a lot? And if that candidate thinks it's permissible (even desirable) to slaughter one particular group legally today, what might he or she think tomorrow? Isn't it possible that the candidate who favors murdering the unborn today may decide that it's acceptable to destroy a segment of our population that includes you tomorrow? Think about it! Sadly, this has happened too many times in history.

So, if a particular candidate is not willing to stand up and boldly defend the most innocent and helpless citizens of their nation, what does that tell you about his or her character? Should believers have a life litmus test for deciding whether or not to vote for a particular candidate? I would say no question about it – yes, we should have a litmus test for life!

Originally posted 10/23/2018

In Genuine Pursuit of Liberty and Justice for All

For the Lord is a God of justice; blessed are all those who wait for him (Isaiah 30:18).

He has told you, O man, what is good; and what does the LORD require of you but to do justice, and to love kindness, and to walk humbly with your God? (Micah 6:8).

For I know how many are your transgressions and how great are your sins – you who afflict the righteous, who take a bribe, and turn aside the needy in the gate. Therefore he who is prudent will keep silent in such a time, for it is an evil time (Amos 5:12-13).

I hate, I despise your feasts, and I take no delight in your solemn assemblies. Even though you offer me your burnt offerings and grain offerings, I will not accept them; and the peace offerings of your fattened animals, I will not look upon them. Take away from me the noise of your songs; to the melody of your harps I will not listen. But let justice roll down like waters, and righteousness like an ever-flowing stream (Amos 5:21-24).

Justice is a very popular word and topic in our culture today. People often speak of wanting liberty, justice, and fair treatment for all. Sadly, true justice isn't really sought after for all. The justice many are seeking is selfish. It is a "justice" that includes some while leaving out others.

Allow me to illustrate. We often quote the words of one of our forefathers of the Revolutionary War era. Patrick Henry nobly and boldly stated, "Give me liberty or give me death!" For the colonists, those were words to cheer and admire. However, the same patriots who would have cheered for Patrick Henry may not have reacted the same way, had a black slave said the same thing. That slave would likely have been shot dead. It's easy to say we want liberty and justice for all, but so often we really only want justice as in "just us." That is, justice for whatever group we choose to include while excluding those we choose to exclude.

Today, many tout justice as a priority for themselves and our culture. On many college and university campuses, students will say that standing up for justice is very important. They will speak out, attend protests, and show great passion in seeking for justice as they see it.

Yet if you ask many of these same students about their thoughts on the importance of standing up for life and standing up for justice for babies in the womb, their loud voices grow strangely quiet. In fact, many of those voices may express anger that you would bring up such a topic. "Well, I believe in reproductive rights for women! How dare you infringe on the rights of women – the right to choose to do what she wants with her body!"

What about justice for the babies? Do they not matter? What happened to justice for all? What they really mean is that they only want justice for people like them or that they like. They don't truly want justice for all. They want it for a specific person or groups of people. But not everyone.

God *is* just, and His Word lets us know that we are all made in His image. So we all have worth and are equal in His sight. Praise God that true justice is defined by Him, not us. Culture's definition of justice may change from one situation to the next, from one group to the next. Someone always seems to be ignored when it comes to justice. Thank God that in His eyes, we all stand equal before Him. God is the Judge and He *is* justice. He will ultimately and finally dispense it perfectly to everyone. In the meantime, if we are going to pursue "justice for all" then let's mean what we say.

Originally posted 8/14/2018

The 'Dear Parent' Letter

She called out of the blue. "My parents have scheduled for me to get an abortion. The abortion is scheduled for tomorrow. I want to keep my baby. Can you help me?" "Shay" was seventeen, still in high school, still very much dependent on and under the care of her dad and mom – and desperate. How she got our phone number, why she chose to call us, how she was funneled to me – we don't know. The best explanation, it seems, is God's grace, His sovereignty, and the Holy Spirit's guidance and direction. She called and was crying out for help. She lived in another state across the country from where our ministry – the American Family Association – is located. What could we do?

In considering this situation, many people in our country do not realize that it is against the law for anyone – a parent, a guardian, a boyfriend, or even a husband – to try to force or coerce an abortion. If a mother is carrying a baby – whether she is 14 years old or 34 years old – and wants to have her baby, it is against the law for anyone to try to force or coerce her to abort her baby. The law is clearly on the mother's side no matter how young she may be!

We immediately emailed Shay a copy of the "Dear Parent" letter that same day. We had her cell phone number, so the following day, after not hearing from her right away, we called her back. We wanted to follow up and check on her. Shay answered the phone. She stated that she was *at* the abortion clinic at that very moment. Her mother had taken her. I thought to myself "Why didn't you show your mother the letter *before* you went to the clinic?" But I did not share my thoughts with Shay. I encouraged her to still show her mother the letter. We then ended our conversation.

Later in the day, Shay called back. I listened to her share the story of how her day went. She said "We didn't get an abortion. I showed Mom and the people at the abortion clinic the letter. The clinic workers let us know that they could not do the abortion in view of my NOT WANTING to have an abortion. Mom was not happy, but the abortion did not happen." Praise God! Praise God! Praise God! Shay went on to say "They did an ultrasound on me. We found out that I was carrying twins." Praise God! The Holy Spirit used the courage of a young lady and this simple letter – the "Dear Parent" letter –that day to save not just one but two babies!

I would encourage every reader to do this, and to do it today. You can read the "Dear Parent" letter below. Get a copy of it. Then read it. Then read it again. Then pray, and ask the Lord who you should send this letter to – either by email or hard copy. Many people – many parents, pastors, youth pastors, high school principals, and counselors – just don't know that this is the law. It is also true that many pregnancy clinic employees, sidewalk counselors, and the like do not know this is the law. Finally, even many persons in law enforcement do not know the law in this matter.

I would encourage you to pray about who you should send a copy of this letter to (letter below). Then send out at least twelve copies or more to people you know who are in places of influence. If you do this, the Lord will use you to save the lives of babies – maybe many babies.

Would you consider doing this? I trust that you will.

The Justice Foundation

Dear Parent (or other concerned persons):

If you are reading this letter, then you have been informed that your minor daughter is pregnant. As difficult and upsetting to you as this information may be, there is hope and help for your daughter and you. Many organizations and groups, including The Justice Foundation and the organization that gave your daughter this letter, are available to help you. You are not alone, and you are not the first to face this issue – there is hope. Positive, healthy outcomes can arise from this situation.

There are important new legal rights that your minor daughter now possesses as a mother that you should know about. Your daughter is now the mother of a child in the womb. Just as you were her mother or father before she was born; she is a mother now, regardless of the circumstances.

As a mother, she has the fundamental right to direct the upbringing and education of her child. *Pierce v. Society of Sisters*, 268 U.S. 510 (1925). That right is hers – not anyone else's. Although you still have the legal duty to care for her, protect her, and provide for her, she has the right to make decisions about the child in her womb, your grandchild.

You (or any other person) may not force, coerce, or pressure your daughter to have an abortion. To do so could subject you to the criminal charge of fetal homicide (killing a baby while

51

still in the womb) in the many states with fetal homicide laws. In other words, any third party (including a relative) who causes the baby to be killed may be guilty of fetal homicide. See, for example, *Lawrence v. State*, 211 S.W.3d 883, 884-85 (Tex. App. – Dallas 2006). You may also be prosecuted under the Federal Unborn Victims of Violence Act.

Even though abortion may be legal, you do not have any right to force, coerce, exert undue influence, or pressure your daughter to have an abortion. The United States Supreme Court makes it clear that an abortion decision by a minor must be hers, that it must be free, independent, voluntary, and non-coerced. See *Bellotti v. Baird*. 443 U.S. 622 (1979). Force, excessive coercion, or duress may also subject you to reporting and prosecution for child abuse. Besides possible criminal prosecution, if you force, coerce, or exert undue pressure, then both you and the abortionist could be held liable for various civil torts, such as battery, negligence, false imprisonment, or other claims.

Some common examples of what would be, in our opinion, excessive coercion, force, duress, or involuntary undue influence might include one or more of the following:

1. "If you have this baby, I am kicking you out of my house." (You do not have to support her child, but you do have to support her just as she has to support her baby. The state and other groups may assist her with support for her child. She also has the right to child support from the father of the child. You and/or she may be eligible for financial assistance from the state and other groups.)

2. "No more talking, I am taking you for an abortion. I have made the appointment."

3. "You are my child and you will do what I say. You will have to have the abortion."

4. "I will beat you within an inch of your life, if you don't stop this nonsense. You are not keeping this baby, and I don't care what you think." (Any threat or infliction of violence is unlawful.)

5. "You are grounded, cut off, and stranded, (or any other punishment) if you don't have this abortion."

The list below includes organizations that may be able to assist you in many ways.

As a Christian organization, we provide our services at no charge to those in need. We have heard from many women who have been forced or pressured to have abortions about the years of devastation resulting from abortion. We hope that this has been helpful to you and desire that you get all the help that you need.

Sincerely,
Allan E. Parker
President
The Justice Foundation

Kathleen Cassidy Goodman
Lead Counsel of the Center Against Forced Abortion
A Project of The Justice Foundation

R. Clayton Trotter
General Counsel
The Justice Foundation
Lead Counsel of the Center Against Forced Abortions
A Project of The Justice Foundation

The Justice Foundation is a non-profit, 50I(c) (3) organization.

The Justice Foundation

8122 Datapoint, Suite 812

San Antonio, Texas 7829

210-614-7157; FAX 210-614-6656; info@uxjf.org;

www.thejusticefoundation.org

www.operationoutcry.org

Originally posted 6/2/2015

Except in the Case of Rape?

The young woman was so excited. After years of searching, waiting, pursuing leads, and being disappointed ... finally, God had blessed her to find and meet her birth mother who was living in a nursing home. The mother was so excited and looking forward to meeting her precious daughter as well.

After visiting, sharing, and spending time, the young woman asked her newly-found mother the question she longed to ask. She wanted to know the truth directly from her mom. She had been told a few years ago by a social worker in what seemed to be a very insensitive manner, "Your mother was raped!"

"Do you mind telling me how was I conceived?" She didn't want to hurt or cause her mom any pain, yet she really wanted to know the truth.

Without hesitation, her mom told her what happened. "I was raped by eight men while walking home from seeing **The Ten Commandments**."

The young woman burst into tears and buried her face in her mother's lap while she knelt in front of her. She patted her new-found daughter on the shoulder and said graciously to her, "Honey stop your crying." That was a long time ago, and I've forgiven those men. And look what God has done. He's brought you back to me. God is faithful!"

Praise God! What a giant woman of faith.

That was a brief retelling of a part of Juda Myers' story in her book *Hostile Conception: Living with Purpose*. It's a story with many insights and truths for the body of Christ to learn about the topic of life and the value of every human being.

It's too common among those who say they stand for life and against abortion, that this statement is made: "I'm against abortion, except in the case of rape." A few questions desperately need to be asked about this statement. What does that statement really mean? Does it mean that babies conceived through rape do not have the same right to live as babies conceived in other circumstances? Should babies conceived in such a violent manner be murdered for the crime of the father? Should a baby conceived through rape be considered somehow second-class because of the tragic circumstance by which he or she was conceived? If someone says that they are pro-life except in the case of rape, does that not make that person pro-choice?

These are just a few tough questions that really need to be asked of persons who say they stand for life, yet make this tragic statement. It seems that when people make that statement, they are basically going against some of the very values that they say they stand for. For instance, the Word of God says, *"You shall not murder."* It does not say, "You shall not murder except in the case of rape." Yet to make the statement "I'm against abortion except in the case of rape" is like saying "I'm against murder except when you want to murder a person who was conceived under this particular circumstance."

The Word of God doesn't change. It is an anchor that helps us in all circumstances know the will of God. The people of God must understand that we are called to *stand* for life. We are not called to stand for life "except in the case of…" We are called to stand for life – period.

Originally posted 8/2/2018

The Tragedy of Wrong Values and Mixed Messages

An abortionist is an individual who kills babies in the womb. He takes the lives of defenseless, harmless innocent babies for any of a number of reasons given by expectant mothers. He does it for a living and typically makes a large income doing this. The word for killing innocent human beings with premeditation is called murder. Sadly, some doctors have decided to become murderers and tragically, it is legal in this nation.

Such an individual spoke to students at Mississippi State University. This particular abortionist says he is a Christian. He is a sad and deceived individual with a very deceptive message that says it is OK to be a "Christian" and murder innocent babies. He is seeking to convince young men and women that it is acceptable to kill innocent babies who have no way of defending or speaking up for themselves. He is basically telling people that one can ignore the clear command in the Ten Commandments that says, *"You shall not murder"* (Exodus 20:13).

On February 14, 2018, our nation witnessed another horrific school shooting (Parkland, FL) in which a young man concluded that killing some of his classmates and school staff was somehow OK. He is now in jail and rightfully so. The word for this is murder. Murder is the taking of innocent life. Abortionists take innocent life regularly. And they get paid a lot of money to do it. Those who take the lives of people who are a little older go to jail.

I witnessed an instance when my wife was ministering to a group of young children. She had asked them what they were thankful for. As they responded, some said the usual things. "I'm thankful for my family, thankful for my mom, thankful for my home." However, two little boys, both younger than seven years of age, each said, "I'm thankful my mama didn't abort me."

Sadly, these two very young boys knew what abortion is. They were grateful that they were not victims of this tragic reality. And, very likely, they knew that possibly a brother or a sister or a cousin or another child is not here because of abortion. So, the questions need to be asked: What kind of world have we made for our children? What messages are they receiving from adults? One message may very well be that adults *keep* some children and adults *kill* some children.

Mother Teresa, in her speech at the 1994 Prayer Breakfast in Washington DC said:

> I feel that the greatest destroyer of peace today is abortion, because it is a war against the child, a direct killing of the innocent child, murder by the mother herself. And if we accept that a mother can kill even her own child, how can we tell other people not to kill one another?

We are told in Proverbs 31:8-9, "*Open your mouth for the mute, for the rights of all who are destitute. Open your mouth,* judge righteously, defend the rights of the poor and needy."

We, the church of Jesus Christ, need to pray very deliberately and passionately for the ending of legalized abortion. We must boldly speak up and speak out for those precious babies who cannot speak for themselves. This needs to become a high priority for the church today. Why? Because the holocaust of abortion has continued to happen on our watch. We need to have the will and the Holy Spirit empowered passion to do our part. With God's help, we can end this.

We encourage and invite all believers to go to themoraloutcry.com and sign the petition. Let us, by God's mercy, wisdom, grace, and power, end legalized abortion.

Originally posted 3/18/2018

Blind Spot or Disconnect?

The health care debate rages on. National and state politicians go back and forth, discussing, arguing, and raging over issues concerning health care – on a national scale and on the state level. Most everyone that you might ask has an opinion on this issue. Why? Well, of course, people's health and health care are *very* important.

Civil rights issues also seem to stay at the forefront of the news. People protesting racism in one form or another make the news every day. Perceived racism, actual racism, discrimination in any form, it seems, "will not be tolerated." Those who perceive racism protest in different ways. Why protest racism perceived or real? Because this issue is *very* important.

Then there are athletes who are choosing to protest by "taking a knee" during the playing of the national anthem. It seems, they are seeking to make a statement though many in our culture don't agree with either their message or methodology. They do it anyway. Why? Because they perceive the issue(s) as *very* important.

We also have entire institutions in our culture which center around protecting people's rights and privileges. Many of them may or may not live up to their name and their so-called cause(s), yet they supposedly exist for the purpose of protecting people's rights. Some include our own U.S. Government, Global Rights, the ACLU, NAACP, etc. People are often adamant about the importance of keeping these entities or institutions in our culture in place in order to protect, safeguard, and advance particular issues and/or rights because they are perceived as *very* important.

Tragically though, there is one people group whose rights regularly get trampled upon, but very few seem willing to protest on their behalf. For this group, the reality is they are simply ignored, and they "don't count." They don't seem to be very important. "What group is that?" you may ask. Children in the womb. Many believe that children in the womb don't count. But the question that must be asked is "Why is this so?"

If people are so concerned about the health care of those who are living, breathing, and walking around in our society, should it not be important for children in the womb as well? If everyone is so concerned about having their civil rights protected, shouldn't the civil rights of children in the womb be protected and respected?

Even if no one else will speak up for these children, the body of Jesus Christ must speak up! We are called to speak up on behalf of the poor, the weak, and the helpless. Proverbs 31:8-9 tells us, "*Open your mouth for the speechless, in the cause of all who are appointed to die.*"

Also, Proverbs 24:11-12 says:

> "*Rescue those who are being taken away to death; hold back those who are stumbling to the slaughter. If you say, "Behold, we did not know this," does not he who weighs the heart perceive it?*"

God sees the unborn as precious, and He sees them as being just as important as any other human being. Therefore, we, the church of Jesus Christ, must do the same. We are called this day to stand for the innocent and speak out on their behalf. Why? Because they, too, are *very* important.

Originally posted 10/25/2017

By the Rivers of Babylon

"By the rivers of Babylon..." begins Psalm 137. This psalm is unique in the book of Psalms. One of the messages it proclaims has to do with the need for steadfastness and perseverance while in captivity. Persevere and don't give up.

Babies in the wombs of their mothers are children, plain and simple. They are extremely young, but children nonetheless. Every human being on this planet was once a very young child just like each of them. The difference between these children and older children is only geography and age.

These very young children are altogether helpless. Basically, if their parents or someone else does not take care of them, they will die. To say they are innocent is a huge understatement. Children in the womb are precious, a blessing, and beautiful.

Today, we find ourselves in a strange land. We live in a strange land where the government refuses to give rights to children in the womb. We live in a land where the government takes taxpayer money to the tune of between 1 and 2 million dollars a day and gives it to a non-governmental organization that concentrates on killing children in the womb – an organization called Planned Parenthood. A strange land. Our government gives extra rights to people who engage in a lifestyle of wicked and deviant sexual practices and then foists those rights and behaviors on everyone. A strange land indeed.

We live in a land where a woman who ran for president stated that children in the womb have *no constitutional rights at all* (so they can be killed at will in our nation). Moreover, she believes the government should pay for the killing of these children.

How sad it is that we live in a world in which at different times in history, people in power have "redefined" certain groups of human beings. In Nazi Germany, the leadership redefined Jews and other groups of people as being useless and a threat to the status quo. This led to the legal taking of their property, rounding up the Jews and certain other groups, arresting them, imprisoning them in concentration camps, and exterminating many of them. What a strange world we live in.

How sad it is that many people in different parts of the world decided that black people from the continent of Africa were not equal to everyone else in the world, and thus could be captured and made into slaves. They were then bought and sold like property and treated as such. And sadly today, the same kind of tragedy still happens to people of many different races and groups through the reality of sex trafficking. And now we live in a place where people kill children before they are born, and call it a right protected by the U.S. Constitution. (Notice that all the people who call this a constitutional right are already born.)

Why do people not see the extreme injustice at work here? Because it's convenient *not* to see them. And the tragic response by too many after being confronted with such realities is "But it's ok to do this because these 'people' are not really people. They are what I have decided they are. They are useless eaters, they are savages, they are animals, and they are fetuses."

We must decide that we will never lose our song! We need to decide to sing loud and clear and boldly and faithfully. Our song is a song of love for all people – children in the womb, people of other colors, and backgrounds, etc. It is also a song of justice.

Our song is a song we are called to sing in righteousness. Let us sing louder and stronger and more courageously than ever before. Our song, justice as defined clearly by the Word of God, is for children in the womb and for everyone else. By the grace of God, let us never lose our song for, in the end, our song will prevail.

Originally posted 7/13/2016

Christmas, Crisis Pregnancy, and Life

Interwoven into the fabric of the wonderful story of Christmas is this unique truth – Christmas and expectant moms go hand in hand. Yes, pregnancy – and specifically crisis pregnancy –has a precious heartwarming tie to Christmas. How so? Actually, it's very obvious. The Christmas story has not just one, but two unusual pregnancies contained within its pages. The specific story within the Christmas story is captured in Luke, chapter 1.

Two mothers meet, come together, and worship and fellowship with each other. One is a teenage mother who has miraculously conceived by a virgin pregnancy. The other mom is one who would normally be classified as a grand or great grandmother based on her age. Yet she is an expectant mom as well.

We often see and think of this story as a warm, lovely story full of peace, joy, and grace. And it is such a story. Yet, the world then, was in so many ways a very harsh, cruel, and perilous world to live in. A world where foreign armies occupied Israel, and kings and nations sometimes killed babies in large numbers. A world where jealousy and disloyalty abounded. Actually, it sounds a lot like the world we live in today.

Our world is one where children can legally be killed

from conception, right up until the moment of delivery. And governments not only do not oppose this; they often finance the carrying out of these tragedies. Often, so-called "experts" advise women to end the lives of their babies in the womb. Time and time again, women are advised to terminate their children based on the "wisdom" or so-called insight of these "experts." However, God's Word is clear: *"You shall not murder"* (Exodus 20:13). God's Word is our guidebook for life. His Word will never lead us to make a bad decision or an unwise decision. God Himself *is* Wisdom. So we need to stand on the wisdom of God's Word which will always lead to blessing, grace, and fulfillment.

In looking at the beautiful and grace-filled story of Christmas, let's consider a "What if?" scenario. What if...

Dr. Yohahn eyed his young patient long and hard. "Young Miss Mary, you are just a teenager. You are not even fully an adult. You really need to think this through. It simply would not be wise to keep this baby. You are not married, you do not know how to tell your betrothed that you are pregnant, and you are just a child yourself. Child, you must listen to wisdom. If you keep this baby your betrothed will surely divorce you and you will become a poor, single mother. No one will want you. You will end up all alone and die in poverty, and no one will ever remember your name. Your child will surely amount to nothing, and no one will ever remember his name either! You must not keep this child! Trust me, I'm a doctor, and we know all about matters like this. Be reasonable! You and the rest of the world will be so much better off if we just quietly do away with this baby. What do you say?"

"Good day, doctor. I am keeping my baby!" replied Mary.

"Mark my words! You and your baby will never amount to anything! And no one will ever even remember your names!"

Dr. Yohahn looked at the elderly woman very curiously. "Listen, Elizabeth. I don't know how in the world this came to be, you pregnant when you are old enough to be someone's grandmother yourself. But let me be straight with you. You really should not keep this child. Being so old and carrying a child means there will be the likelihood that there will be something wrong with the child. A woman your age could not have a healthy child! The child will probably have many problems! At your age both you and the child could die during labor! Be reasonable! Make it easy on yourself and the baby, and just get rid of it. If the child does survive childbirth, his life will never amount to anything. He will probably grow up to be a burden on society and nothing else! Mark my words. I am a physician, and we understand these kinds of things! Don't you think you should do away with the baby?"

"Good day, doctor. I am keeping my baby!" replied Elizabeth.

"Suit yourself, old woman! But know this: You and the whole world will regret your decision! I'm a professional, and I know very well how these kinds of things turn out!"

Hmm.

Originally posted 12/15/2014

The Epitome of Racism

So, whatever you wish that others would do to you, do also to them, for this is the Law and the Prophets (Matthew 7:12).

The verse above is known as the Golden Rule, and if everyone lived by it, the world's major problems would be solved – including racism.

Racism. We hear the word every day it seems. This leader, that politician, this celebrity, that group is racist! In this day and time, "racist" is one of the ultimate tags that are to be avoided like the plague.

What is the definition of "racism?" Webster calls it "a belief that race is the primary determinant of human traits and capacities and that racial differences produce an inherent superiority of a particular race." Another definition from Merriam-Webster states that racism is "racial prejudice or discrimination."

Meanwhile, abortion is the number-one cause of African-American deaths in the United States. Is this deliberate and massive slaughter of a single race not a clear demonstration of the epitome of racism? This is not the enslavement of black people but rather an attempt to exterminate them all.

It's genocide!

Who is the number-one provider of abortions in the United States? Planned Parenthood. No other group provides more abortions in our nation than they do.

So where is the outrage toward Planned Parenthood? Where are the angry cries of racism? Where is the media attention, and why is no one labeling this genuinely racist group as what it is to its core?

Planned Parenthood has a large number of abortion clinics throughout the nation, two-thirds of which are in minority neighborhoods. Planned Parenthood kills more black babies through abortion in four weeks than the KKK killed over the span of 150 years. Yet for some reason, many in our culture and in the media consistently give them a pass when it comes to the designation of racism.

In her published article titled "Woman, Morality, and Birth Control," Margaret Sanger (the founder of Planned Parenthood) states the following:

> We should hire three or four colored ministers, preferably with social-service backgrounds and with engaging personalities. The most successful educational approach to the Negro is through a religious appeal. We don't want the word to go out that we want to exterminate the Negro population, and the minister is the man who can straighten out that idea if it ever occurs to any of their more rebellious members.

I don't believe it would be difficult to classify such remarks as racist. Not only was Margaret Sanger a racist, but she was passionately zealous about this cause.

Planned Parenthood and those who support the organization to this day continue to lift up Margaret Sanger as a heroine and honor her legacy. What a tragedy. If ever there was an organization that had thoroughly earned the designation of being racist, Planned Parenthood is in the running for the number-one spot.

Think long and hard about the following story in which Mr. KKK and Mr. PP meet one day and have a long discussion:

Mr. PP: *Mr. KKK, you've been around a long time, and you have quite a legacy of fighting and getting rid of black folks. But I need to inform you that you've been going about it all wrong.*

Mr. KKK: *How so? I think I've been pretty successful. We have gotten rid of a lot of black folks in our time.*

Mr. PP: *Let me educate you. Your perspective is OK; your methodology is the problem. You're going about it all wrong.*

Mr. KKK: *OK, Mr. PP, educate me.*

Mr. PP: *I'll do just that. You have been opposing black folks and getting rid of them for more than 150 years. You don't like them and they don't like you. Look at me and my associates. Black folks don't like you, but they love us. They like us and consider us their friends. We've managed to encourage them to think we want what is best for them.*

Mr. KKK: *Hmm. You've got a point there.*

Mr. PP: *There are laws against getting rid of black folks the way you've done it – by lynching, murder, etc. We were wise and cunning enough to make it legal to get rid of black folks by our methodology: abortion. You and your associates can potentially go to jail for using your methods. Me and my* *associates are heralded as compassionate heroes and heroines for using our methods.*

Mr. KKK: *You know, you've got a point.*

Mr. PP: *You and your associates have to chase and capture your victims. We, on the other hand, have persuaded these folks to bring their little ones to us and let us get rid of them for them. And they pay us to do it!*

Mr. KKK: *Man, I would have never thought of such a plan! You guys make us look like amateurs!*

Originally posted 1/23/2018

Righteous Leaders,
Righteous Laws, and Life

The legalization of abortion was a tremendous error on the part of the U. S. Supreme Court. It should have never happened. Once the door was opened and our nation considered it a constitutional right, many people chose to have an abortion only because it was legal. Nearly five decades after the 1973 *Roe v. Wade* decision, more than 60 million unborn babies have been brutally murdered.

Righteous laws are very important. They make all the difference in the world. They clearly help people in their thoughts, perspectives, and in making decisions with regard to a given issue. So, to have righteous leaders who wisely make righteous laws is vital – it is absolutely critical to everything in life.

Too often, both young people and adult, in seasons of immaturity or difficulty, have made decisions to do things that were unwise in the moment. And often later, these persons tremendously regret their decisions. Many would never have made those choices if there had been some kind of roadblock in place – likea law against it.

Righteous laws help and encourage society to make wise decisions. Righteous laws help steer us in God-honoring directions. They help and encourage us to do things that are in everyone's best interest. Righteous laws are extremely important to our nation and culture.

God clearly speaks to the issue of life in His Word. He wants everyone to honor life. One of the Ten Commandments says *"You shall not murder."* This means that no one is to take the life of innocent persons. In what situation is it permissible to purposely ignore and disobey what God clearly tells us not to do? Obviously, there are no such situations, and that includes abortion.

All righteousness flows from God. Every word in the Bible is righteous and right. If a society bases its laws on the Word of God, it helps to establish a righteous community. And God's righteousness is good for everyone. So, if we are wise as a nation, we will continually seek to put righteous leaders in office who know and reverence the Word of God. We will endeavor to support leaders as they make righteous laws for our land addressing issues such as the sanctity of life.

Sometimes people say, "I'm against abortion, but I don't want to make it illegal because I believe in a woman's right to choose." Well let's look at this point of view. Consider a few questions. Why would someone be personally against abortion? If it is a good thing, it should be fully supported. Why was abortion against the law until 1973? Why do so many of those who have had one try so hard to hide the fact? If it's good, shouldn't we be very upfront about it, support it, and talk openly about it? If you personally believe that it's wrong and destructive, why would you support it for others but not for yourself? These and many other questions should help us to see that there is much self-deception and misinformation about the issue of life in our society.

God has spoken, and if we are to honor Him, we are to

accept and stand on His Word. He has told us, *"You shall not murder"* (Exodus 20:13). He has also told us *"choose life, that you and your offspring may live"* (Deuteronomy 30:19). Believers should not support what God has clearly said is wrong. Let's choose to get on God's side. Let us pray fervently that God would put more and more righteous leaders in office. Let us pray fervently for our leaders that they will seek to honor God in their decision making. And let us pray and believe God for the end of legalized abortion.

Originally posted 1/18/2018

Some Mass Murders Don't Matter

The shooting in Orlando in June of 2016 was a horrible tragedy. A person full of darkness murdered 49 individuals mercilessly. It should be in the news cycle 24/7 as it has been. It seems that we hear of mass shootings and before we have comprehended the magnitude and devastation of one, another has taken place. Human beings dying needlessly at the hands of hate-filled killers. Every shooting, whether it was on a school campus, in a public building, a nightclub, or even a church – has been tragic, saddening, and disturbing.

Yet strangely we are relatively silent about one type of mass killing. This kind of mass killing, for some unusual reason, doesn't stir the culture and our society like these mass shootings do. This type of mass killing is "different." It's not "the same." In fact, this type of mass killing is considered so "unimportant" it doesn't even make the news. Yet sadly, those who have died as a result of these mass killings far outweigh the numbers in the tragic shootings that periodically make the news.

I am speaking of the mass murder called abortion. Tragically, the moment many read the word "abortion," the reaction is "Oh, why are you even bringing up abortion? It's a completely different matter. I am offended that you are even comparing the two issues at all."

Yet the question must be asked: "Why? Why don't we care about the babies? Why are they so unimportant to us and our society? Why do we ignore the huge numbers of children who have died by abortion?" These acts of terrorism must be dealt with directly and decisively.

In a December 2, 2013, USA Today article, it was stated that more than 900 people died in mass shootings in the U.S. over the last seven years. A New York Times article from September 24, 2014, stated that from December 2000 to 2013, 1,043 people in the U.S. were wounded or killed by active shooters attempting to kill people in a confined or populated area. Sadly, almost a thousand babies are murdered *every day* in this country at the hands of the terrorists performing abortions. Yet it doesn't even make the news.

The Word of God clearly tells us, *"You shall not murder."* The proper translation means "You shall not take innocent life." So, this means whether people are in a public place, a workplace, a night club, in a church building – or in the womb – innocent life must not be taken. All are human beings made in the image of God. Not one of those persons is more important or less important than the others.

We, as God's people, must speak up for babies in the womb. They are the one group that cannot speak up, protest, march, or stand for themselves. Let's boldly get busy! Let's bring this tragedy to an end!

Originally posted 6/22/2016

Safe, Legal, and Rare?

When politicians say they want abortion to be safe, legal, and rare, they are being deceptive. Why?

1. Abortion is the deliberate taking of an innocent life and is, therefore, murder. God will certainly forgive this sin (if forgiveness is sought), but the sin being forgiven is not an error of judgment but the sin of murder.

2. How can something be safe if the end result of doing it is the death of a human being? There is nothing "safe" about the deliberate taking of innocent human life.

3. If taking an innocent life is deemed acceptable for one reason, what is to prevent it from being taken for a whole host of reasons? There are any number of situations that might be deemed "helpful" or "convenient" when measuring the value of someone's life. It is both cruel and nonsensical to say abortion should be safe, legal, and rare.

Obviously and tragically, abortion has not been rare. Over the last 40+ years more than 60 million babies have been aborted in our nation. That is not an indication of abortion being rare by any stretch of the imagination. More than 2,000 abortions per day is overwhelming! And to make sure it continues to thrive, the U.S. government has been giving Planned Parenthood almost two million dollars a day, making it the biggest abortion provider in the world demonstrating that it has little concern with making abortion rare.

When you hear politicians speak of "safe, legal, and rare" keep in mind they are really saying "I support the legalized killing of innocent babies as widely as we choose to carry it out."

We are not deceived by politicians who want abortion to be safe, legal, and rare. That is just code for us to leave the heavy lifting of moralizing and legislating to them. It sounds nice but it means nothing. The truth is that person actually wants a woman to be able to have an abortion *any time* she wants one.

Originally posted 1/20/2016

The Danger of Sleeping in Church

Acts 20:7-12 reveals an interesting account about sleeping in church that has implications and lessons we can use today. They allow us to stay awake at the wheel so we can drive forward with the purpose God has given us for the church.

In this account, the Apostle Paul is in Troas preaching late into the night. At this particular gathering is a young man named Eutychus. He is apparently sitting in a window sill and falls "into a deep sleep." If that wasn't bad enough, he then tumbles out of the third story window of the building and dies. Paul goes down to the young man, and with the Spirit of God, raises Eutychus from the dead.

What are the lessons to be drawn from this story?

One lesson is if you are going to sleep in church, don't sleep in the church window. Another lesson might be if you are going to sleep in the church window, be sure that it is not the window of a three-story church. Or, if you are going to sleep in the window of a three-story church, be sure it has very strong screens on the windows.

On a serious note, what are the implications of a story like this found in the Word of God?

One of the truths to be learned is that if you are in the church you really do need to be wide awake. You need to be sober-minded, alert, and discerning of what the church is and what we are called to be doing. We need to be passionate about understanding our mission and bold about carrying it out.

We really don't need to be asleep at the wheel in church. We are called to be wide awake and bold about our calling.

What is the bold mission that we are to be about? We are to passionately and aggressively seek to:

1. Proclaim the gospel and make disciples (Matthew 28:19-20; Mark 16:15). Too many believers are doing little if anything to help be witnesses and spread the gospel of Jesus Christ in the world.

2. Proclaim and live the truth, helping to set people free from the bondage of sin (Luke 4:18-19).

3. Love, reach out, embrace, and minister to a world of hungry and hurting people in need (Matthew 25:31-40).

4. Speak the truth with courage and faith to a world that largely does not value truth.

We are called to carry the light of the truth of God's Word to a world steeped in darkness. We are to proclaim the Word of God to people who will sometimes question whether or not God even exists.

We are called to help the world hear and know the truth that sets people free. We are called to share truth, such as God made us male and female, and those are the only genders. God can save and deliver a person from the bondage of lifestyles that don't align with His Word. We are not to compromise with darkness.

We are called to be wide awake and proclaim to the world the truth that clearly says, "You shall not murder." Too many in our culture, including church leaders, are ignoring words that cause death the same as murder like "abortion," "reproductive rights," and "euthanasia." Sin cannot be hidden by substituting words.

We are called to be wide awake while boldly and unapologetically saying "Thus says the Lord" because it is the Word of God that has the answer to all of the world's problems. We are not to conform to the world, but we are to be instruments in the hands of God showing the world the will of God and the blessings that follow accomplishing His will (Romans 12).

It is impossible to be bold for Christ if we are asleep, not paying attention to the details of His inerrant, authoritative decrees. It's time to wake up and recognize who we are and who we belong to. Let's wake up, come alive, and be about our Father's business.

Originally posted 10/8/2018

Selective Outrage

The terrorist group ISIS continues to carry out evil acts of cruelty and killing. We are angered and appalled at the things we have seen and/or heard that they do. Their actions are so vile and cruel (decapitations, immolations, rape, etc.) one wonders if there is even a shred of humanity left within them. "What horrible human beings they are!" we may react.

They go into public places, catch people unaware, and slaughter them in large numbers. It is a very cowardly form of warfare, yet it is clearly a tactic that incites fear in the hearts of people all over the world. YouTube videos are used to show horrific acts of execution and barbarism the likes of which most people in the world would never see without today's technology and addiction to social media.

The immorality and barbarism of ISIS are almost daily in our faces. And we are both horrified and outraged... rightfully so. And yet, here in America, we kill babies in far greater numbers than the victims of ISIS and in just as barbaric ways. The fear of ISIS has created a global refugee crisis. People are fleeing in huge numbers in countries where ISIS is known to be established. Yet the babies in the wombs of their mothers in our nation cannot run and they cannot hide. And we slaughter them by the thousands *every day*.

ISIS has a systematic method of financing their fear-inducing and killing operations all over the world. In the U.S., we have Planned Parenthood, which has a very "efficient" baby-killing operation that functions daily. And our government uses our tax money to help fund Planned Parenthood to the tune of between one and two million dollars *every day*. Planned Parenthood can insist they provide numerous services to women all they want but their main reason for existence is to kill babies, plain and simple.

ISIS beheads its enemies. What does Planned Parenthood do? It kills babies, sometimes by tearing them limb from limb. Sometimes they use a vacuum so strong that it tears the baby apart. Sometimes they poison and burn the babies in the womb. And they don't stop there. They even sell the baby parts for profit! They sell whole babies, babies' livers, hearts, lungs, etc. Even ISIS doesn't do that! Planned Parenthood makes ISIS look like a bunch of amateurs! ISIS has killed thousands, and Planned Parenthood has killed tens of millions!

How can we condemn ISIS and not even defund Planned Parenthood? How can we demand the world rid itself of ISIS while *paying* Planned Parenthood to do the same? How is it that what ISIS is doing is evil, but what Planned Parenthood is doing is a service?

Originally posted 12/2/2015

Planned Parenthood: An Evil Legacy

The revelation of a video that implicates Planned Parenthood in the selling of baby body parts is chilling. It points to practices and actions that are hard to imagine that anyone would actually do to a human being. Yet, tragically, for Planned Parenthood, this kind of activity is nothing new. Planned Parenthood is simply a very wicked and evil organization. It's what it is and what it has been from the beginning.

The undercover video (by the Center for Medical Progress) may have put Planned Parenthood back in the spotlight, but it's been this kind of organization all along. Planned Parenthood kills babies. It is a high priority for them. They particularly target minorities and especially the African-American community. They strategically place the majority of their clinics in predominantly black neighborhoods. Why? Because they have a very wicked and racist agenda. Their goal is to get rid of groups that they consider undesirable. This has been one of their goals from their beginning.

Consider some quotes from the lips of the founder of Planned Parenthood, Margaret Sanger:

> We don't want the word to go out that we want to exterminate the Negro population, and the minister is the man

who can straighten out that idea if it ever occurs to any of their more rebellious members.

In *The Pivot of Civilization,* Sanger shared some of her thoughts concerning immigrants, the poor, and other "undesirables." She stated, "They are ... human weeds, 'reckless breeders,' 'spawning ... human beings who never should have been born." One of Sanger's goals through the use of birth control was to prevent the birth of individuals whom she considered "unfit" for society. In *Woman and the New Race,* Sanger stated, "Birth control is nothing more or less than the facilitation of the process of weeding out the unfit, of preventing the birth of defectives or of those who will become defective." This is the legacy of Margaret Sanger and Planned Parenthood. This is who they were then, and it is who they are now.

As an African American pastor, my suggestion to our community is to spend significant time, energy, and effort on confronting Planned Parenthood and those who support them. Addressing issues such as the Confederate flag and statues of civil war "heroes" has a place. But I believe that much more concern, effort, and energy needs to be focused on standing against this living, breathing, vigorously racist organization called Planned Parenthood. We say the KKK is an enemy and rightly so. Yet Planned Parenthood kills more black babies in two weeks, than all of the black people the KKK has killed in 150. Many of us in the black community need to wake up and look at who our most dangerous enemies are. It's not mainly the white hood. It's Planned Parenthood.

Originally posted 7/16/2015

Men and Abortion

In our culture, it's commonly said that abortion and abortion rights are about a woman having the right to choose what to do with her own body. This is one of the ongoing claims of pro-choice people who are sold out to the tragedy of abortion. Well, if the concern is really about a woman's "right" to choose, then consider a huge reality that is being glaringly overlooked in our culture today.

Statistically speaking, men are the driving force behind many abortions. Allow me to share a scenario that is tragically very common. Too often, in our culture, a man, upon learning that his girlfriend is pregnant, will become upset. Often he will become angry and ask a typically stupid question: "How did this happen?" His actual thoughts are "Why didn't you do all you could to prevent this with all the birth control methods and means there are?" He will then selfishly make other statements like:

"I am not ready to be a daddy!"

"We can't afford a baby!"

"How could you have let this happen?"

Then, too often, the next reaction is "You will get an abortion. Do you understand? There is no need for discussion."

And in many cases, the girlfriend does exactly what her boyfriend demands.

Though it is very often stated that this issue is about a woman's right to choose, is she choosing? In many such cases, you have a woman that either *wants* to keep her baby, or you have a woman who is on the fence and undecided. Then, upon receiving the reaction of her boyfriend, she will decide "I better do what he says." Again, this situation is extremely common in our culture. Even though it is said that it is her "right to choose," too terribly often, she is being coerced or more or less forced to have an abortion against her will.

Now, it is actually against the law to force or coerce a woman to have an abortion if she wants to keep her baby. Tragically though, many women don't know that this is the law. Many of them do not realize that the law is on their side. Many men do not know this is the law either. Also, sadly, many men don't care.

So, it's not hard to see that, though many claim they want to maintain a woman's right to choose, this is actually not the issue. Time and time again in this sad situation, the woman is not "choosing" at all. The man is.

There is an overwhelming need for persons that know and understand the law in this situation to help inform more people of the law. It can be done by word of mouth obviously, yet two very helpful resources are the "Dear Client" letter or "Dear Parent" letter, (found at **www.thejusticefoundation. org** or see p.39). Churches and schools should get copies of these items or similar resources to help people come to know the law.

Men have too often taken away women's right to choose life. They have done too often exactly what they should not have done – demanded an abortion. This situation needs to end. The ignorance and selfishness of our culture have already done way too much damage. Any concerned individual can help spread the word.

Originally posted 7/22/2014

Living Biblically

In the beginning was the Word, and the Word was with God, and the Word was God. He was in the beginning with God. All things were made through him, and without him was not any thing made that was made. In him was life, and the life was the light of men. The light shines in the darkness, and the darkness has not overcome it (John 1:1-5).

Your word is a lamp to my feet and a light to my path (Psalm 119:105).

...and how from childhood you have been acquainted with the sacred writings, which are able to make you wise for salvation through faith in Christ Jesus. All Scripture is breathed out by God and profitable for teaching, for reproof, for correction, and for training in righteousness, that the man of God may be complete, equipped for every good work (2 Timothy 3:15-17).

"For best results, follow the instructions of the manufacturer."

These are words we often find in the instruction manual

or manuscript that comes with a purchase that needs to be assembled. This is very common. That's true because usually, the one who made or "created" the appliance or item knows better than others how to put it together and/or how it should function or operate correctly.

God, our heavenly Father, is the "manufacturer", the Maker and Sustainer of life and of all people. He created the whole world and all the people in it. As both the Creator and Sustainer of life, He created things and knows how they were created to work best - most fruitfully and correctly.

At times, the statement is made "The problem with life is that it doesn't come with an instruction manual." Well, I beg to differ. Oh, yes it does! That instruction manual is called the Bible. It is the written Word of God. The Bible is the Word of God in print. The Word of God is God's will, His counsel, and His wisdom. The Word of God is God's heart and His truth – for all the world and for all of life.

God's Word covers all of life in its wisdom and counsel. Every concern, every issue, and every topic is addressed in some way. In either direct statement or principle, God's Word covers everything. God's Word is the key to all of life. It's the key to everything.

As believers, it should be our desire and our intention to live following and walking in the wisdom of God's precious Word. We are called to live a lifestyle of consistently choosing to follow the guidance God's Word gives us. That is how we live biblically. The Bible, God's Word, is the guidebook for all of life for us. As we live by and follow the guidance found in God's Word, we are living biblically.

In order to live biblically, believers would be wise to pursue doing at least two things faithfully with God's Word in their lives. Believers should:

1. Read and meditate on the Word of God daily.

2. Obey the Word of God.

Living biblically simply means that a believer is consistently listening to the Word of God, and consistently doing what it says. He or she is guided by the direction, instructions, and counsel given in God's holy Word. For the believer, the Bible is not simply a book that decorates our coffee tables and sits handsomely on our shelves as a symbol of the spirituality of one's family. It's our guidebook for all of life, our roadmap for the entire journey.

So when a believer reads in the Word of God, *"Be kind to one another..."* then he or she needs to purposely choose to walk in kindness. When believers are mean, impatient, grouchy, and hard to get along with, they are not living biblically. If a believer obeys this command, he or she would be considerate of the life, feelings, and concerns of others, and act accordingly.

When an individual reads *"You shall not steal,"* yet consistently steals items from the company where he or she works, that person is not living biblically. To obey that command would be to respect the possessions and ownership of others.

When a person reads in the Word of God, *"You shall not commit adultery,"* yet he or she lives an immoral lifestyle, getting involved sexually with one or more persons to whom they are not married, that person is not living biblically. Or if a person gets involved in homosexual sin in any form, that individual is not living biblically.

When an individual reads *"You shall not kill,"* yet willfully goes to an abortion clinic to have an abortion, or pays for someone to have an abortion, that person or those persons are not living biblically. Or if a person drives an individual to a clinic to assist them, that person is not living biblically in this situation.

It is very critical that we as Christians faithfully pursue living out the guidance and direction God's Word gives us. That's what it is for – to give us guidance and direction in order to be successful in our lives.

Living biblically is its own reward. Obedience to the Word of God leads to a life of greater blessing and freedom. Obedience is always followed by blessing. To disobey the Word of God always leads to loss one hundred percent of the time. Disobedience will always cause you loss in some way. It simply does not pay to disobey God's Word.

So, living biblically is its own reward. Obedience to God always leads to blessing. Every believer is called to live biblically. We are called to be diligent students who continually listen to the Word of God. And we are to be faithful to live out that which we read and learn. And know that the call to live a biblical lifestyle is a call that God gives to all of His children.

Originally posted 3/6/2015

An Interview With
Pastor Joseph Parker

Dr. Robert Youngblood, associate editor of The Stand, talked with Pastor Joseph Parker for more of his insights on the biblical foundation for life.

American Family Association (AFA): Pastor Joseph, you've been writing for many years on abortion and the value of life. Do you remember how you were first drawn to write and preach about this issue so much?

Pastor Joseph Parker (JP): I remember it was in the early 1990s, and I had been a pastor for about 16 or 17 years. I had an experience where it was like a mantle the Lord put on me to wear. It's like a burden for the life issue.

I think it's an honor to be able to serve the Lord in any capacity. However, it was like God placed a burden on me to really begin to address this issue, to be an advocate for the life issue in different venues.

Down through the years, pastorally, this topic has gotten me in trouble more than any other – but in a good way. Because if you get in trouble for Jesus, it's an honor. But the topic has caused more repercussions than any other one I can think of.

As I wrote the first few articles, I was grateful for the opportunity to begin to share and address it. I've come to see very clearly that pastors in particular, and the church as a whole, really need a lot of help to fully understand this issue from God's heart and God's perspective. It seems like many pastors are afraid of the issue. They don't know how to really deal with it and address it.

Obviously when you're helping the pastors, you're helping the church.

AFA: What are some of the Ten Commandments which you see being broken related to this issue of abortion?

JP: Well, really, all of them.

Obviously the first one, you should have no other gods before me.

For some people, they've clearly made abortion a god, an idol. People will fight tooth and nail to support it, to defend it, to fund it to the point where it is crazy.

But it's not really crazy. It's demonic. The lies of abortion are like the thief which kills, steals, and destroys. Jesus came to offer life instead. Christians need to be more passionate about our God than pro-abortionists are about their god because we have a greater cause.

Of course, the very obvious one is the Sixth Commandment, you shall not murder. The King James Version says you shall not kill, but a proper translation is you shall not murder, which means you shall not take innocent life. And how much more innocent can a person be than a baby in the womb?

So abortion is clearly a violation of God and His Word. Sadly, there have been millions, over 60 million since *Roe v. Wade* in 1973. So those two commandments clearly and powerfully stand out.

AFA: What hope does God offer to a woman who has had an abortion or a man who has encouraged a woman to have an abortion?

JP: Well, you know, the Word is really full of hope for people at every stage of this issue. We hope if someone is considering abortion, she would come to recognize this is not honoring to God, and this is a precious child. However, some people have already gone down that road and had an abortion.

One great hope I have is for people to recognize Scripture as in 1 John 1:9: *"If we confess our sins, He is faithful and just to forgive us our sins and to cleanse us from all unrighteousness."* Without question, we serve a God full of lovingkindness and mercy and forgiveness.

There is so much collateral damage from abortion. When the church preaches and teaches truth and helps us see it from God's perspective, not only are babies saved, but mothers are saved. Marriages are saved, and families and clans are saved, too. So, when the church does its job, everybody benefits. You know when we speak the truth in love, everybody gets blessed.

AFA: Have you ever been accused of not speaking the truth in love regarding abortion? And how is someone able to determine whether they are speaking in love or not?

JP: I think as believers we just need to walk in an intimate relationship with the Lord Jesus and ask Him to help us to be faithful, to walk in love. This is important because it is not hard to get in your flesh – if you allow yourself – even when you are speaking truth.

The reality is all of us are in desperate need of the love and mercy and forgiveness of Jesus for so many different things. 1 John 1:8 says, "If we claim to be without sin, we deceive ourselves and the truth is not in us." So, we don't have a place to feel like *I can condemn you, but I am mighty and righteous.* No, all of us need the love and mercy and forgiveness of Jesus. We are not in a position to be condemning toward others.

I recall an instance where a young school teacher had come to me and said, "Pastor, I need to talk to you." She didn't even want to say it with her mouth. She wrote on a piece of paper, "Last Thursday I had an abortion."

My thoughts were not thoughts of condemnation but of great compassion. This is something that is devastating to the person emotionally, spiritually, and mentally. I just really felt for her, for what she was going through. To this day, all these years later, when I last saw her, she has grown, but it seems like she's still dealing with it.

So, it is very sad to see when a person has not allowed the Lord to bring healing and forgiveness to herself.

Without question, my hope is that God will always help me to have the heart of compassion He wants me to have because it is not my job to condemn. It is my job to share the love of Christ and the truth spoken in love.

AFA: When you talk about us not allowing God to heal, several articles mention the seven different ways we can be immersed in God's Word. Since God's Word and His people are some of the ways He brings healing, would you review those briefly?

JP: One of my favorite verses is Psalm 119:105, *"Your word is a lamp to my feet and a light for my path."* With this, I like to remind believers of how we can use the Word of God daily: We can read it, hear it, believe it, speak it, obey it, pray it, and meditate on it.

It's good for us to understand this: God's Word is Jesus and Jesus His Word. We spend lots of time reading and meditating on the Word of God. It's an appointment time with Jesus who knows how to work on us, to mold us, and to shape us.

The Word of God can minister healing and wholeness to us in a way that no one else and nothing else can, because God's Word is Jesus. And there's power – power to heal, power to forgive, power to bless, power to mold us and make us what we need to be. We all need Jesus to work on us, and the results are always good.

I think of two different individuals, Lee Strobel and Josh McDowell. Both men were once atheists. Each had the intention to disprove Jesus. But they made the mistake of reading the Bible. It got to them. And both of them got saved and accepted the Jesus they were trying to disprove because they found themselves in God's Word and exploring the truth behind it.

This is all just a reminder of the power of the gospel, the power of Jesus at work in His people through His Word.

AFA: Pastor Joseph, what else would you like to share related to your hopes for this book?

JP: I hope that believers who read it will be set on fire with the Holy Spirit to become a much more faithful and passionate ambassador for the Kingdom of God and with it also, the life issue. There's such a need for many more believers to courageously address this issue in love and with the truth of God's Word.

About Pastor Joseph Parker Sr.

Joseph Parker is a servant of the Lord Jesus Christ, a Bible teacher, and a pastor. He is married to Pastor Birdie Parker. He is on staff with American Family Association, serving as host of the radio broadcast **The Hour of Intercession** on the American Family Radio network. He coordinates pro-life outreach for the ministry of AFA. He and his wife Birdie host The Festival for Life, a pro-life multimedia event, in local churches.

He seeks to help believers make the *means of grace* – John Wesley's phrase for spiritual disciplines – a critical part of their lives and lifestyles.

The Parkers have six children and three grandchildren. He has served as a pastor for most of the last 44 years, and is currently pastor of Bethlehem A.M.E. Church in Winona, Mississippi.